Changing Weather

Nellie Wilder

sun

clouds

showers

rain

storm

hail

showers

rainbow

Let's Do Science!

What happens when the weather changes? Try this.

What to Get

- ❏ paper cup with holes in the bottom
- ❏ shoe box filled with dirt
- ❏ water

What to Do

1 Make hills and valleys in the dirt.

2 Slowly pour water on the scene through the cup.

3 Put the scene in the sun.

4 How does the weather change the land?

Glossary

hail—rain that has turned to ice

showers—light rain

storm—heavy rain with lightning and thunder

Index

21

Your Turn!

Have you seen a storm?
Write and draw to tell
about it.

Consultants

Sally Creel, Ed.D.
Curriculum Consultant

Leann Iacuone, M.A.T., NBCT, ATC
Riverside Unified School District

Jill Tobin
California Teacher of the Year
Semi-Finalist
Burbank Unified School District

Publishing Credits

Conni Medina, M.A.Ed., *Managing Editor*
Lee Aucoin, *Creative Director*
Diana Kenney, M.A.Ed., NBCT, *Senior Editor*
Lynette Tanner, *Editor*
Lexa Hoang, *Designer*
Hillary Dunlap, *Photo Editor*
Rachelle Cracchiolo, M.S.Ed., *Publisher*

Image Credits: pp.2–17 Stephanie Reid and Lexa Hoang; pp.18–19 (illustrations) Rusty Kinnunen; all other images from Shutterstock.

Library of Congress Cataloging-in-Publication Data

Wilder, Nellie, author.
  Changing weather / Nellie Wilder.
    pages cm
  Summary: "It is time to learn how the weather can change."— Provided by publisher.
  Audience: K to grade 3.
  Includes index.
  ISBN 978-1-4807-4531-5 (pbk.) —
  ISBN 978-1-4807-5140-8 (ebook)
1. Weather—Juvenile literature.
2. Readers (Primary) I. Title.
  QC981.3.W535 2015
  551.5—dc23
                              2014008931

Teacher Created Materials
5301 Oceanus Drive
Huntington Beach, CA 92649-1030
http://www.tcmpub.com
ISBN 978-1-4807-4531-5
© 2015 Teacher Created Materials, Inc.
Made in China
YiCai.032019.CA201901471